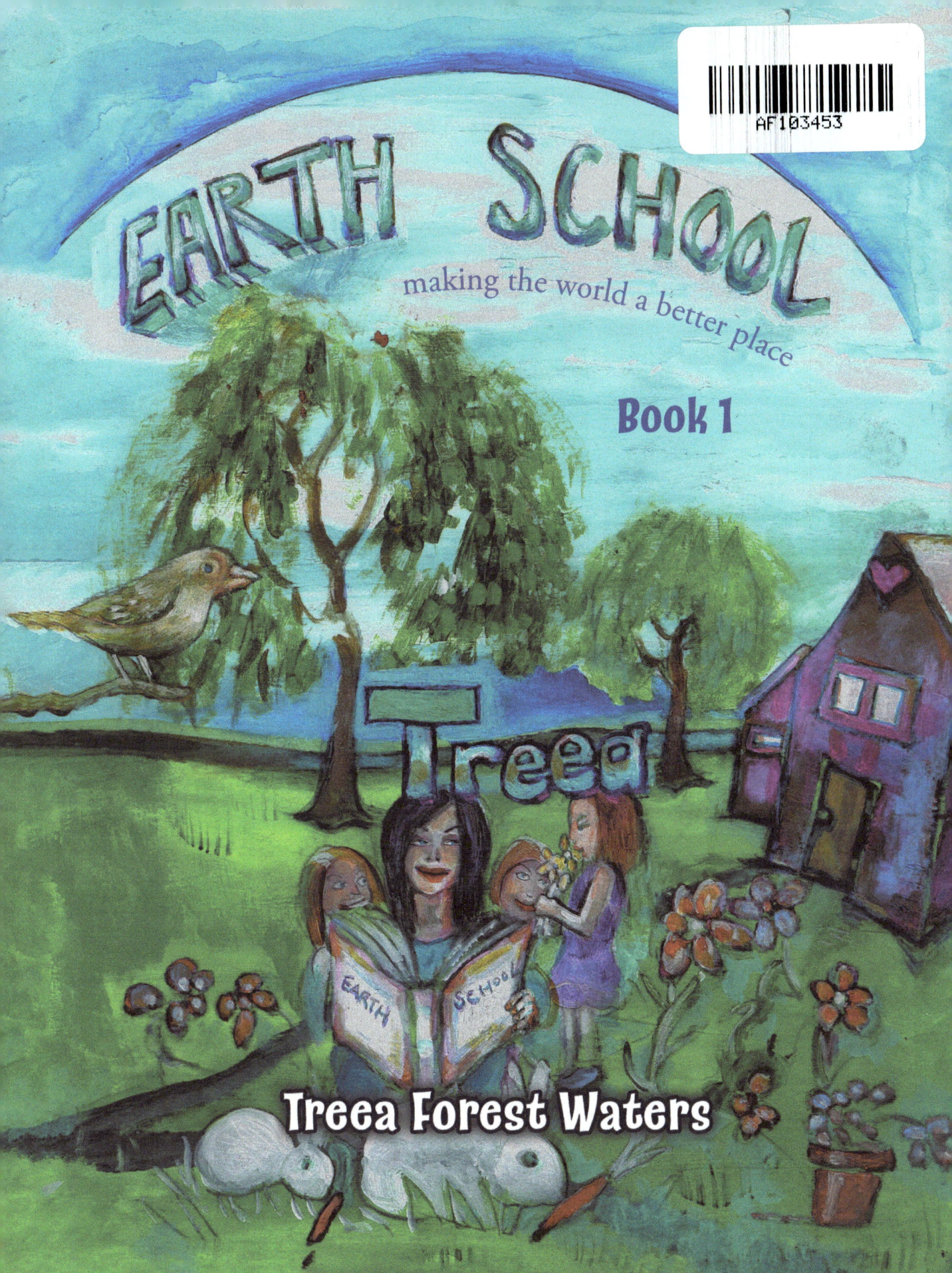

Book 2 Coming Soon

Earth School
Copyright © 2019 by Treea Forest Waters

All rights reserved. No part of this publication may be reproduced, distributed, or transmitted in any form or by any means, including photocopying, recording, or other electronic or mechanical methods, without the prior written permission of the author, except in the case of brief quotations embodied in critical reviews and certain other non-commercial uses permitted by copyright law.

treea.ca
treeafarm.com

Tellwell Talent
www.tellwell.ca

ISBN
978-0-2288-0937-1 (Paperback)
978-0-2288-1811-3 (eBook)

One of my favourite places in the world is Clear Waters. It is a very special place. There are large fields, gardens, clear lakes, rivers, ponds and good clean air.

Our town of Clear Waters is a place where kind, compassionate and caring people live and help one another. They are environmentally conscientious and do their best to protect the planet.

The people believe in self-sustainability by living off the land, growing their own food and minimizing their environmental footprint.

This is me, Treea and my brother Earth, we love to write stories about our adventures. We love to learn and are excited to go to our school called Earth School.

At Earth School all our lessons pertain to real life. We learn these life skills through hands on learning and experiential learning.

There are a variety of subjects at our school that we can choose, based on our interests, our learning styles and our readiness.

Each individual is responsible for showing respect and care of each other and the environment. What responsibilities do you have at school?

Our library is filled with many books that support our learning. I love to learn about the Seven Grandfather Teachings: Love, Respect, Courage, Honesty, Wisdom, Humility and Truth.

One of my favourite subjects is gardening. We have a garden at our school where we grow our own food.

We plant the seeds in our classroom and then transplant them in our garden. We grow vegetables, fruit, plants and trees.

What are your favourite vegetables? Can you name a vegetable that grows under the ground and one that grows above ground?

What is your favourite fruit that grows in your area?

Which of these plants do you find in your area? Always remember to leave flowering plants in the ground so that our bees can thrive and pollinate our crops.

We grow and cook our own food with the help of community volunteers. By not bringing packaged lunches we also reduce waste.

As well as planting gardens with vegetables and fruit, we learn how to plant and harvest trees. Trees are a very important renewable resource.

Look at how many different types of trees there are. Here are just a few! How can we use trees? How can we replace them?

At Earth School, children are focused on helping their community. As well as tending gardens, children have tree routes where they care for the growth of the trees.

Families are also involved in the school community. They help us learn about replenishing the planet and making sure that everything that is taken is replaced.

My favourite tree is the apple tree. We even have several apple orchards at Earth school. Making apple treats and pies is always fun. Even our animals enjoy apples.

Composting is very important.
We use our compost for our gardens to provide more nutrients to our soil.

Beehives are also very important.
Did you know that bees are endangered?
We need to save the bees as they pollinate our crops and plants.

At Earth School, everyone helps out.
We support our farmers and each other.
Through our work at school and in the community
we learn to get along and make friends.

Now that you have seen the importance of protecting our planet what part can you play in helping the environment and in becoming self-sustainable?

Thank you for joining me on our journey through Earth School. For more adventures, follow me at treea.ca or treeafarm.com.

www.ingramcontent.com/pod-product-compliance
Lightning Source LLC
LaVergne TN
LVHW070119080526
838200LV00080B/4699